HAL•LEONARD
INSTRUMENTAL
PLAY-ALONG

FLUTE

AUDIO
ACCESS
INCLUDED

PLAYBACK+
Speed • Pitch • Balance • Loop

CONTEMPORARY BROADWAY

T0081880

Audio arrangements by Peter Deneff

To access audio, visit:
www.halleonard.com/mylibrary

Enter Code
6896-5782-6693-0739

ISBN 978-1-5400-5925-3

HAL•LEONARD®

Visit Hal Leonard Online at
www.halleonard.com

Contact us:
Hal Leonard
7777 West Bluemound Road
Milwaukee, WI 53213
Email: info@halleonard.com

In Europe, contact:
Hal Leonard Europe Limited
42 Wigmore Street
Marylebone, London, W1U 2RN
Email: info@halleonardeurope.com

In Australia, contact:
Hal Leonard Australia Pty. Ltd.
4 Lentara Court
Cheltenham, Victoria, 3192 Australia
Email: info@halleonard.com.au

CONTENTS

ALL THAT MATTERS
from FINDING NEVERLAND

Flute

Words and Music by ELIOT KENNEDY
and GARY BARLOW

5

DEFYING GRAVITY
from the Broadway Musical WICKED

FLUTE

Music and Lyrics by
STEPHEN SCHWARTZ

ME AND THE SKY
from COME FROM AWAY

Flute

Music and Lyrics by IRENE SANKOFF
and DAVID HEIN

MICHAEL IN THE BATHROOM

from BE MORE CHILL

FLUTE

Words and Music by
JOE ICONIS

MY SHOT
from HAMILTON

Flute

Words and Music by LIN-MANUEL MIRANDA
with ALBERT JOHNSON, KEJUAN WALIEK MUCHITA,
OSTON HARVEY, JR., ROGER TROUTMAN,
CHRISTOPHER WALLACE

13

ONCE UPON A DECEMBER
from the Broadway Musical ANASTASIA

FLUTE

Words and Music by LYNN AHRENS
and STEPHEN FLAHERTY

PRACTICALLY PERFECT

from MARY POPPINS

Flute

Music by GEORGE STILES
Lyrics by ANTHONY DREWE

PROUD OF YOUR BOY

from ALADDIN

FLUTE

Music by ALAN MENKEN
Lyrics by HOWARD ASHMAN

RIGHT HAND MAN

from SOMETHING ROTTEN!

FLUTE

Words and Music by WAYNE KIRKPATRICK
and KAREY KIRKPATRICK

SEIZE THE DAY

from NEWSIES THE MUSICAL

FLUTE

Music by ALAN MENKEN
Lyrics by JACK FELDMAN

SHE USED TO BE MINE

from WAITRESS

FLUTE

Words and Music by
SARA BAREILLES

STUPID WITH LOVE

from MEAN GIRLS

Flute

Words by NELL BENJAMIN
Music by JEFFREY RICHMOND

WAVING THROUGH A WINDOW

from DEAR EVAN HANSEN

Flute

Music and Lyrics by BENJ PASEK
and JUSTIN PAUL

WHEN I GROW UP
from MATILDA

FLUTE

Words and Music by
TIM MINCHIN

WHERE DID THE ROCK GO?

from SCHOOL OF ROCK

FLUTE

Music by ANDREW LLOYD WEBBER
Lyrics by GLENN SLATER

HAL•LEONARD INSTRUMENTAL PLAY-ALONG

The Beatles

All You Need Is Love • Blackbird • Day Tripper • Eleanor Rigby • Get Back • Here, There and Everywhere • Hey Jude • I Will • Let It Be • Lucy in the Sky with Diamonds • Ob-La-Di, Ob-La-Da • Penny Lane • Something • Ticket to Ride • Yesterday.

_____	00225330	Flute	$14.99
_____	00225331	Clarinet	$14.99
_____	00225332	Alto Sax	$14.99
_____	00225333	Tenor Sax	$14.99
_____	00225334	Trumpet	$14.99
_____	00225335	Horn	$14.99
_____	00225336	Trombone	$14.99
_____	00225337	Violin	$14.99
_____	00225338	Viola	$14.99
_____	00225339	Cello	$14.99

Chart Hits

All About That Bass • All of Me • Happy • Radioactive • Roar • Say Something • Shake It Off • A Sky Full of Stars • Someone like You • Stay with Me • Thinking Out Loud • Uptown Funk.

_____	00146207	Flute	$12.99
_____	00146208	Clarinet	$12.99
_____	00146209	Alto Sax	$12.99
_____	00146210	Tenor Sax	$12.99
_____	00146211	Trumpet	$12.99
_____	00146212	Horn	$12.99
_____	00146213	Trombone	$12.99
_____	00146214	Violin	$12.99
_____	00146215	Viola	$12.99
_____	00146216	Cello	$12.99

Disney Greats

Arabian Nights • Hawaiian Roller Coaster Ride • It's a Small World • Look Through My Eyes • Yo Ho (A Pirate's Life for Me) • and more.

_____	00841934	Flute	$12.99
_____	00841935	Clarinet	$12.99
_____	00841936	Alto Sax	$12.99
_____	00841937	Tenor Sax	$12.95
_____	00841938	Trumpet	$12.99
_____	00841939	Horn	$12.99
_____	00841940	Trombone	$12.99
_____	00841941	Violin	$12.99
_____	00841942	Viola	$12.99
_____	00841943	Cello	$12.99
_____	00842078	Oboe	$12.99

The Greatest Showman

Come Alive • From Now On • The Greatest Show • A Million Dreams • Never Enough • The Other Side • Rewrite the Stars • This Is Me • Tightrope.

_____	00277389	Flute	$14.99
_____	00277390	Clarinet	$14.99
_____	00277391	Alto Sax	$14.99
_____	00277392	Tenor Sax	$14.99
_____	00277393	Trumpet	$14.99
_____	00277394	Horn	$14.99
_____	00277395	Trombone	$14.99
_____	00277396	Violin	$14.99
_____	00277397	Viola	$14.99
_____	00277398	Cello	$14.99

Movie and TV Music

The Avengers • Doctor Who XI • Downton Abbey • Game of Thrones • Guardians of the Galaxy • Hawaii Five-O • Married Life • Rey's Theme (from *Star Wars: The Force Awakens*) • The X-Files • and more.

_____	00261807	Flute	$12.99
_____	00261808	Clarinet	$12.99
_____	00261809	Alto Sax	$12.99
_____	00261810	Tenor Sax	$12.99
_____	00261811	Trumpet	$12.99
_____	00261812	Horn	$12.99
_____	00261813	Trombone	$12.99
_____	00261814	Violin	$12.99
_____	00261815	Viola	$12.99
_____	00261816	Cello	$12.99

12 Pop Hits

Believer • Can't Stop the Feeling • Despacito • It Ain't Me • Look What You Made Me Do • Million Reasons • Perfect • Send My Love (To Your New Lover) • Shape of You • Slow Hands • Too Good at Goodbyes • What About Us.

_____	00261790	Flute	$12.99
_____	00261791	Clarinet	$12.99
_____	00261792	Alto Sax	$12.99
_____	00261793	Tenor Sax	$12.99
_____	00261794	Trumpet	$12.99
_____	00261795	Horn	$12.99
_____	00261796	Trombone	$12.99
_____	00261797	Violin	$12.99
_____	00261798	Viola	$12.99
_____	00261799	Cello	$12.99

Songs from Frozen, Tangled and Enchanted

Do You Want to Build a Snowman? • For the First Time in Forever • Happy Working Song • I See the Light • In Summer • Let It Go • Mother Knows Best • That's How You Know • True Love's First Kiss • When Will My Life Begin • and more.

_____	00126921	Flute	$14.99
_____	00126922	Clarinet	$14.99
_____	00126923	Alto Sax	$14.99
_____	00126924	Tenor Sax	$14.99
_____	00126925	Trumpet	$14.99
_____	00126926	Horn	$14.99
_____	00126927	Trombone	$14.99
_____	00126928	Violin	$14.99
_____	00126929	Viola	$14.99
_____	00126930	Cello	$14.99

Top Hits

Adventure of a Lifetime • Budapest • Die a Happy Man • Ex's & Oh's • Fight Song • Hello • Let It Go • Love Yourself • One Call Away • Pillowtalk • Stitches • Writing's on the Wall.

_____	00171073	Flute	$12.99
_____	00171074	Clarinet	$12.99
_____	00171075	Alto Sax	$12.99
_____	00171106	Tenor Sax	$12.99
_____	00171107	Trumpet	$12.99
_____	00171108	Horn	$12.99
_____	00171109	Trombone	$12.99
_____	00171110	Violin	$12.99
_____	00171111	Viola	$12.99
_____	00171112	Cello	$12.99

Wicked

As Long As You're Mine • Dancing Through Life • Defying Gravity • For Good • I'm Not That Girl • Popular • The Wizard and I • and more.

_____	00842236	Flute	$12.99
_____	00842237	Clarinet	$12.99
_____	00842238	Alto Saxophone	$12.99
_____	00842239	Tenor Saxophone	$11.95
_____	00842240	Trumpet	$12.99
_____	00842241	Horn	$12.99
_____	00842242	Trombone	$12.99
_____	00842243	Violin	$12.99
_____	00842244	Viola	$12.99
_____	00842245	Cello	$12.99

HAL•LEONARD®